Joy Richardson

Gareth Stevens Publishing
MILWAUKEE

For a free color catalog describing Gareth Stevens' list of high-quality books and multimedia programs, call 1-800-542-2595 (USA) or 1-800-461-9120 (Canada). Gareth Stevens Publishing's Fax: (414) 225-0377.

Gareth Stevens Publishing would like to thank Gundega Spons of the Milwaukee Art Museum for her kind and professional help with the information in this book.

Library of Congress Cataloging-in-Publication Data available upon request from publisher. Fax (414) 225-0377 for the attention of the Publishing Records Department.

ISBN 0-8368-2629-9

This North American edition first published in 2000 by
Gareth Stevens Publishing
1555 North RiverCenter Drive, Suite 201
Milwaukee, Wisconsin 53212 USA

Original edition © 1997 by Franklin Watts. First published in 1997 as *Changing Colour* by Franklin Watts, 96 Leonard Street, London, EC2A 4RH, United Kingdom. This U.S. edition © 2000 by Gareth Stevens, Inc. Additional end matter © 2000 by Gareth Stevens, Inc.

Gareth Stevens Editor: Monica Rausch
Gareth Stevens Cover Designer: Joel Bucaro
U.K. Editor: Sarah Ridley
U.K. Art Director: Robert Walster
U.K. Designer: Louise Thomas

Photographs: © British Museum pp. 4-5; reproduced by courtesy of the Trustees of the National Gallery, London Lotto/Family Group pp. 6-7, Meléndez/Still Life pp. 8-9, Turner/Fighting Téméraire pp. 10-11, 29 (detail), Monet/Water-Lily Pond pp. 14-15, 28 (detail), Seurat/Bathers at Asnières cover, pp. 16-17, 26 (detail), van Gogh/ Sunflowers pp. 18-19; © RMN/Renoir/Dancing at the Moulin de la Galette pp. 12-13/© RMN/Gauguin/ The White Horse pp. 20-21, 29 (detail); © Succession André Derain/DACS 1997, The Pool of London/© Tate Gallery, London, pp. 22-23; © Succession Kandinsky/DACS 1997 Cossacks © Tate Gallery, London, pp. 24-25.

Printed in Mexico

1 2 3 4 5 6 7 8 9 04 03 02 01 00

Contents

For additional information about the artists and paintings, see pages 30-31.

Hunting Birds
from Nebamun's tomb

Nebamun is out hunting. These bright colors were painted over three thousand years ago.

The painter probably had black, white, red, yellow, and blue paint to use.

Which colors did the painter mix to make these browns?

Look at the color patterns in . . .

the cat's fur,   the bird's feathers,

and the fish's scales.

Giovanni della Volta and His Family

painted by Lorenzo Lotto

Lotto used his best colors for the
foreground of this painting.

Colors were made from rocks, plants, or insects.
The best blues and reds cost a lot of money.

Look at the rosy red and rich blue clothes . . .

and the brilliant colors
in the tablecloth.

In the background,
the sea is a duller,
less costly blue.

Still Life with Oranges and Walnuts
painted by Luis Meléndez

In this collection of ordinary things,
the colors are arranged to look good together.

Look at the browns in . . .

a barrel,

a box,

a jug,

and some walnuts.

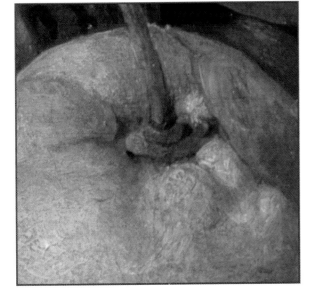

Are the oranges all
the same color?

How many different
greens can you see?

Fighting Téméraire
painted by J. M. W. Turner

Sunset colors set the scene,
as the old ship is towed away.

Look at the sunset colors . . .

reflected in the water . . .

and on the black
steam tugboat.

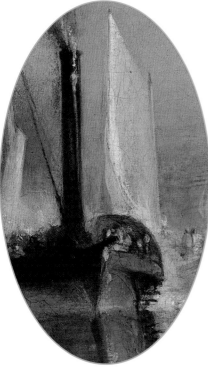

The old
sailing ship
is tinged
with gold.

Can you see the tiny,
pale, new moon?

Le Moulin de la Galette

painted by Pierre-Auguste Renoir

Renoir discovers dancing colors at
a sunlit party in the open air.

Look at the dappled colors where sunshine filters through the trees.

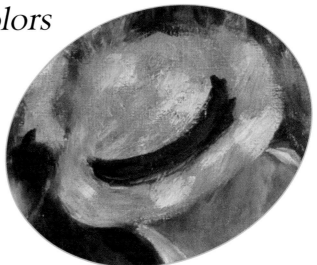

The dress shimmers and gleams.

The face softly glows.

Blurry brush strokes make colors quiver in the light.

Renoir used many colors.

The Water-Lily Pond
painted by Claude Monet

Monet painted his pond again and again,
watching how colors changed with the light.

What colors are the willow trees?

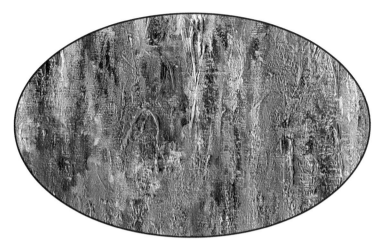

Sunshine stripes
the green with gold.

What color is
the bridge?

What color is the water?

Reflections shine
between the lily pads.

Purple shadows
hide the white
of the bridge.

Bathers at Asnières
painted by Georges Seurat

This painting is like a mosaic,
filled with thousands of strokes of color.

Look at the colors in . . .

shining water,

grass
on the
bank,

and smoke
in the sky.

What colors can you
find in the shadows?

Sunflowers

painted by Vincent van Gogh

Van Gogh was excited by the
blazing yellow colors of sunflowers.

He painted the golden flowers with a lemon background. How many yellows can you see?

Strokes of thick paint make drooping petals

and bumpy seed heads.

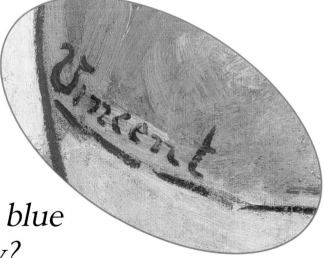

Where can you find blue setting off the yellow?

The White Horse
painted by Paul Gauguin

Gauguin paints a magical world of animals, plants, and people in colorful harmony.

The white horse mirrors
the colors of the forest.

The red horse stands
out against the green.

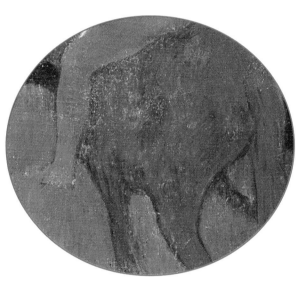

The gray horse blends
into the shadows.

Flowers bloom in the
dark undergrowth.

The Pool of London
painted by André Derain

Derain used strong, bright colors
in this scene to make a lively painting.

Look at his colorful patchwork.

He put colors
together carefully.

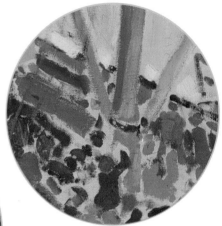

Look for pairs of
red and green,

blue and
orange,

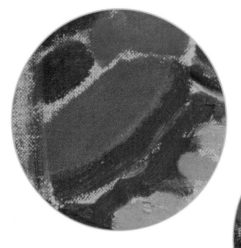

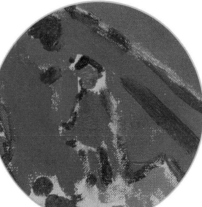

and yellow
and mauve.

The colors in these
pairs are opposite
colors. When painted
close together, they make
one another brighter.

He set everything
off with green sea
and sky.

Cossacks
painted by Wassily Kandinsky

Soldiers are fighting a battle.
Colors and lines capture the feeling.

Fur-hatted soldiers march with lances.

Swords slash, and horses clash.

Birds fly off
in a flurry.

Look at the rainbow
bridging the valley.

Painting with Color

Color circle

Red, yellow, and blue are called primary colors. Other colors fit between them, like the colors of a rainbow.

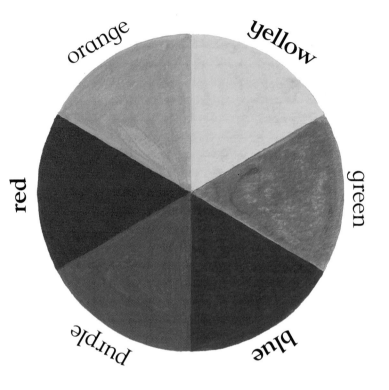

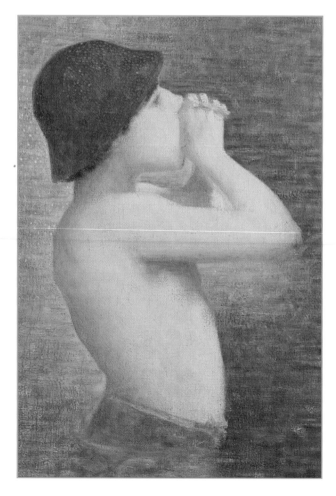

Try painting this color circle. Start with the primary colors. Then mix each pair of primary colors together to make the color between them.

Opposites, like blue and orange, can make each other look brighter.

For help, look back at pages 16 and 22.

Color count

How many colors can you make by mixing two colors together?

Try painting a plain yellow stripe. Add a little red to the yellow for the next stripe, and a little more red each time, to make as many different colors as you can.

Try adding white and black to one color, such as blue, to make lighter and darker shades.

For help, look back at pages 12 and 14.

Making brown

Gather an assortment of
brown objects. Using red,
yellow, blue, black, and
white paints, try to mix
colors that match
each brown.

For help, look back at pages 4, 8, and 18.

Merging colors

Strokes of color painted close
together merge when seen
from a distance.

Try painting grass or leaves
on a tree with small brush
strokes of different colors.

For help, look back at pages 14 and 16.

Color and emotions

Colors affect our feelings, or emotions.
Colors help set the mood in paintings.

Draw a simple picture twice.
Paint one picture with colors to
make it look cheerful and paint
the other with gloomy colors.

For help, look back at
pages 10, 18, and 20.

Color change

Create your own color
scheme. Paint a shell, a
face, a tree, or a cloudy
sky with different colors
that look good together.

For help, look back at
pages 20, 22, and 24.

More about the paintings in this book

■ **Hunting Birds** *(page 4)*

Nebamun was an official in ancient Egypt. This scene was painted on a wall of his tomb around 1400 B.C. It shows him in a papyrus boat on the marshes with his wife and daughter. The painter used colors made from powdered minerals.

■ **Portrait of Giovanni della Volta and His Family** *(page 6)*

Lorenzo Lotto (about 1480-1556) worked in Venice. He wrote in his account book that this portrait was "judged for quality and the finest colors" and valued at fifty ducats. The best colors were expensive and hard to find. The finest blue, made from the mineral lapis lazuli, cost more than gold.

■ **Still Life with Oranges and Walnuts** *(page 8)*

Luis Meléndez (1716-1780) came from a family of Spanish painters. He tried, but failed, to gain a post at the royal court, and he died a poor man. He was a brilliant still life painter, including the smallest details in his paintings. You can even see the woodworm holes in this table.

■ **Fighting Téméraire** *(page 10)*

Joseph Mallord William Turner (1775-1851) was impressed by the sight of this old sailing ship being towed away by a modern steam tug. The ship had fought in the Battle of Trafalgar. The colors he used set the mood, as the sunset salutes a splendid past, and the new moon rises over a changing world.

■ **Le Moulin de la Galette** *(page 12)*

Pierre-Auguste Renoir (1841-1919) was a French impressionist painter. This picture is a kaleidoscope of shifting colors. Unlike painters in earlier times, Renoir and his friends could choose from a huge range of inexpensive, machine-made colors and carry their paints around with them in metal tubes.

■ **The Water-Lily Pond** *(page 14)*

Claude Monet (1840-1926) set out to paint an *impression* of what he really saw, rather than what he specifically knew or remembered. He built this Japanese-style bridge over the pond in his garden, and he painted the same view many times, delighting in the ever-changing colors.

■ Bathers at Asnières *(page 16)*

This huge painting is 6.5 feet x 10 feet (2 meters x 3 meters), and the foreground figures are almost life-size. Georges Seurat (1859-1891) planned every detail from sketches. He achieved his color effects by patiently laying countless strokes of blended color beside one another. Later, he began to make his paintings from dots of pure color.

■ Sunflowers *(page 18)*

Vincent van Gogh (1853-1890) wanted to paint pictures of sunflowers to decorate his house at Arles in France, which he moved into in 1888. Over the summer, he made five paintings with yellow backgrounds. Colors carried strong feelings for van Gogh. He often used yellow in his paintings and usually balanced it with blue.

■ The White Horse *(page 20)*

Paul Gauguin (1848-1903) left France in 1891 and went to live on the South Pacific island of Tahiti, where he painted this picture. He believed that artists should study nature but paint from their imagination. He chose colors to capture the mood and to make the picture look good, rather than to simply show what he saw.

■ The Pool of London *(page 22)*

André Derain (1880-1954) was French, but he painted this picture in England. He put Tower Bridge in the background as a helpful landmark. Derain was interested in new theories about color contrasts, and he used these theories to make the painting more vivid. People were shocked at first and called painters like Derain *Les Fauves*, or "the wild beasts."

■ Cossacks *(page 24)*

Wassily Kandinsky (1866-1944) was Russian. In 1911, he made this painting of Cossacks (Russian cavalry) fighting. Kandinsky was an early abstract painter, exploring the way colors and forms can show emotions without representing recognizable objects. Here, you can pick out soldiers and weapons, and the mood of a conflict is created by the arrangement of colors, shapes, and lines.

Glossary

abstract: difficult to understand; not relating to anything in the real world.

dappled: spotted or patched with a color that differs from the background.

filters: passes through a screen, or filter, letting only a small amount through.

foreground: the part of a picture or painting that seems to be the closest to the viewer.

impressionists: painters from the 1870s who believed in painting the first "impression" of their subjects in short dabs of colors, conveying reflected light more than a realistic image.

mosaic: a decoration made by placing small pieces of colored materials side by side to form a picture or pattern.

primary colors: the colors red, yellow, and blue, which can be mixed to make all other colors.

shimmers: reflects or shines with a wavering, flickering light.

still life: a picture of objects that are arranged in a setting and don't move.

Web Sites

The Art Room
www.arts.ufl.edu/art/rt_room/
@rtroom_home.html

ToonaCat's Coloring & Online Painting
www.toonacat.com/kids/coloring/
jcolfram.html

Due to the dynamic nature of the Internet, some web sites stay current longer than others. To find additional web sites, use a reliable search engine with one or more of the following keywords: *art, impressionism, Claude Monet, painting,* and *Vincent van Gogh.*

Index

SBC